Global Governance: The Role of G-7, G-8, and G-20

ROBERTO MIGUEL RODRIGUEZ

Copyright Page

TITLE: Global Governance: The Role of G-7, G-8, and G-20

1ST Edition

Copyright @ 2023

ISBN: 9798223917076

Table of Contents

Global Governance: The Role of G-7, G-8, and G-20

By Roberto Miguel Rodriguez

Chapter 1: The Economic Importance and the Future of the G-7, G-8, and G-20

The Evolution and Purpose of the G-7, G-8, and G-20

Introduction:

In the realm of global economic governance, the G-7, G-8, and G-20 have played pivotal roles in shaping policies, promoting cooperation, and addressing key economic challenges. This subchapter explores the evolution and purpose of these influential groups and their impact on various facets of the global economy.

1. The Economic Importance and the Future of the G-7, G-8, and G-20:

The G-7, initially formed in 1975, comprises the world's most advanced economies. Over time, it expanded to include Russia, forming the G-8. Subsequently, recognizing the need for broader representation, the G-20 was established in 1999, encompassing both developed and emerging economies. This section discusses the economic significance of these groups and their future relevance in an increasingly interconnected world.

2. The Impact of G-7, G-8, and G-20 on International Trade and Globalization:

The G-7, G-8, and G-20 have been instrumental in shaping global trade policies, reducing barriers, and fostering economic integration. This section highlights their contributions to international trade liberalization, the promotion of open markets, and the challenges posed by protectionism and trade disputes.

3. The Role of G-7, G-8, and G-20 in Addressing Global Economic Inequality and Poverty:

Addressing global economic inequality and poverty has been a key concern for these groups. This section explores their efforts in promoting inclusive growth, poverty alleviation, and social development through various initiatives, such as the Millennium Development Goals and the Sustainable Development Goals.

4. The Influence of G-7, G-8, and G-20 on Global Financial Stability and Regulation:

The G-7, G-8, and G-20 have played crucial roles in maintaining global financial stability, especially during times of economic crises. This section examines their efforts in strengthening financial regulations, enhancing transparency, and coordinating responses to financial shocks, with a particular focus on the 2008 global financial crisis.

5. The Environmental Sustainability Agenda of G-7, G-8, and G-20 and Its Impact on Future Economic Development:

Recognizing the importance of environmental sustainability, these groups have increasingly incorporated climate change and sustainability into their agendas. This section examines their efforts in promoting green growth, combating climate change, and transitioning towards a more sustainable and resilient global economy.

6. The Role of G-7, G-8, and G-20 in Shaping Global Economic Policies and Governance:

These groups have served as influential platforms for shaping global economic policies and governance mechanisms. This section discusses their role in coordinating macroeconomic policies, fostering cooperation on financial matters, and shaping global economic architecture.

7. The Importance of G-7, G-8, and G-20 in Promoting Innovation and Technological Advancements:

Innovation and technological advancements are critical drivers of economic growth. This section explores the contributions of these groups in fostering innovation, research, and development, as well as promoting digital transformation and technological cooperation.

8. The Future Prospects of G-7, G-8, and G-20 in Light of Emerging Economies and Regional Blocs:

As emerging economies gain prominence, questions arise about the future relevance and effectiveness of these groups. This section examines the challenges and opportunities that emerging economies and regional blocs present for the G-7, G-8, and G-20, and their potential for collaboration and cooperation.

9. The Potential Challenges and Opportunities for G-7, G-8, and G-20 in a Post-Pandemic World:

The COVID-19 pandemic has posed unprecedented challenges to the global economy. This section discusses how these groups can address the economic fallout, promote recovery, and strengthen global health systems to prevent future pandemics.

10. The Role of G-7, G-8, and G-20 in Addressing Global Health Crises and Pandemics:

The G-7, G-8, and G-20 have played significant roles in addressing global health crises and pandemics, including HIV/AIDS, Ebola, and COVID-19. This section explores their contributions in terms of funding, research cooperation, and strengthening health systems.

11. The Implications of G-7, G-8, and G-20 on Regional Economic Integration and Cooperation:

These groups have influenced regional economic integration and cooperation by fostering dialogue, promoting trade agreements, and supporting regional development initiatives. This section examines their impact on regional economic dynamics and the potential for deeper integration.

Conclusion:

The G-7, G-8, and G-20 have evolved to address the ever-changing global economic landscape. As platforms for dialogue and coordination, they have played crucial roles in addressing economic challenges, promoting sustainable development, and shaping global economic governance. However, their future prospects depend on their ability to adapt to emerging economies, address new challenges, and foster inclusive and cooperative approaches to global economic governance.

The Significance of G-7, G-8, and G-20 in Global Economic Governance

Introduction:

Global economic governance plays a crucial role in shaping the future of our interconnected world. This subchapter will delve into the significance of G-7, G-8, and G-20 in this realm, addressing the concerns and interests of economists and diplomats. We will explore the economic importance and future prospects of these groups, their impact on international trade and globalization, their role in addressing global economic inequality and poverty, as well as their influence on financial stability, environmental sustainability, global economic policies, innovation, and regional cooperation.

The Economic Importance and the Future of G-7, G-8, and G-20:

The G-7, G-8, and G-20 serve as vital platforms for economic cooperation and coordination among the world's leading economies. With their combined economic power, these groups play a pivotal role in shaping global economic policies and governance. However, the emergence of new regional blocs and emerging economies poses challenges to the relevance and effectiveness of these groups. We will explore their future prospects in light of these changes and discuss potential opportunities for collaboration.

The Impact of G-7, G-8, and G-20 on International Trade and Globalization:

The G-7, G-8, and G-20 have a significant impact on international trade and globalization. Their discussions and agreements on trade liberalization, market access, and regulatory frameworks shape the global economic landscape. We will analyze the influence of these groups on trade policies, investment flows, and the reduction of trade barriers, highlighting the benefits and challenges they bring to global economic integration.

The Role of G-7, G-8, and G-20 in Addressing Global Economic Inequality and Poverty:

Addressing global economic inequality and poverty is a pressing challenge for the world. The G-7, G-8, and G-20 have the potential to play a transformative role in this regard. We will explore the initiatives and policies undertaken by these groups to promote inclusive growth, reduce poverty, and narrow the wealth gap. Additionally, we will assess their effectiveness and discuss potential areas for improvement.

The Influence of G-7, G-8, and G-20 on Global Financial Stability and Regulation:

Maintaining global financial stability and regulating the financial sector is crucial for sustainable economic development. The G-7, G-8, and G-20 have taken significant steps to enhance financial regulation, strengthen oversight, and coordinate responses to financial crises. We will examine their influence on global financial stability, the development of the regulatory framework, and the challenges they face in maintaining a resilient and well-regulated financial system.

The Environmental Sustainability Agenda of G-7, G-8, and G-20 and its Impact on Future Economic Development:

Recognizing the urgency of addressing environmental challenges, the G-7, G-8, and G-20 have incorporated environmental sustainability into their agendas. We will discuss their efforts to promote sustainable development, combat climate change, and transition towards a green economy. Moreover, we will analyze the impact of these initiatives on future economic development, exploring the potential benefits and challenges they pose.

Conclusion:

The G-7, G-8, and G-20 hold significant importance in global economic governance. Their role in addressing economic inequality, promoting trade and globalization, ensuring financial stability, fostering innovation, and tackling environmental challenges cannot be understated. However, as the world evolves, these groups must adapt and collaborate with emerging economies and regional blocs to maintain their relevance and effectiveness. The challenges and opportunities they face in a post-pandemic world and their contribution to global health crises and regional economic integration should be carefully considered for a prosperous and sustainable future.

The Role of G-7, G-8, and G-20 in Shaping Global Economic Policies

In the ever-changing landscape of global economic governance, the G-7, G-8, and G-20 have emerged as critical forums for addressing pressing economic challenges and shaping global economic policies. As economists and diplomats, it is crucial for us to understand the role of these groups and their impact on various aspects of the global economy.

The Economic Importance and the Future of the G-7, G-8, and G-20

The G-7, consisting of the world's largest advanced economies, has historically played a significant role in setting the global economic agenda. However, with the rise of emerging economies, the G-20, which includes both advanced and developing nations, has gained prominence as a more inclusive platform for economic cooperation. This raises questions about the future relevance and effectiveness of the smaller G-7 and G-8 groups.

The Impact of G-7, G-8, and G-20 on International Trade and Globalization

One of the key areas where the G-7, G-8, and G-20 have exerted influence is international trade and globalization. These groups have been instrumental in promoting free trade, reducing trade barriers, and addressing trade imbalances. Their collective efforts have shaped trade agreements, such as the World Trade Organization (WTO), and have had a significant impact on global trade flows and economic integration.

The Role of G-7, G-8, and G-20 in Addressing Global Economic Inequality and Poverty

Another important aspect of the G-7, G-8, and G-20's work is addressing global economic inequality and poverty. These groups have recognized the importance of inclusive growth and poverty reduction, and have launched initiatives to promote sustainable development and social inclusion. By coordinating policies and sharing best practices, they aim to create an equitable and prosperous global economy.

The Influence of G-7, G-8, and G-20 on Global Financial Stability and Regulation

Global financial stability and regulation have been key concerns for the G-7, G-8, and G-20. In the wake of the 2008 financial crisis, these groups have played a crucial role in coordinating responses, designing regulatory frameworks, and strengthening financial institutions. Their efforts have been instrumental in preventing future crises and promoting stability in the global financial system.

The Environmental Sustainability Agenda of G-7, G-8, and G-20 and Its Impact on Future Economic Development

Recognizing the urgent need to address climate change and promote environmental sustainability, the G-7, G-8, and G-20 have placed a strong emphasis on the environmental agenda. They have worked towards promoting clean energy, reducing carbon emissions, and supporting sustainable development. Their policies and initiatives have significant implications for future economic development and the transition to a green economy.

In conclusion, the G-7, G-8, and G-20 play a crucial role in shaping global economic policies and governance. They influence international trade, address economic inequality and poverty, promote financial stability and regulation, drive environmental sustainability, and foster innovation and technological advancements. However, the future prospects of these groups are not without challenges. The rise of emerging economies and regional blocs, the post-pandemic world, and the need to address global health crises and pandemics pose both opportunities and potential obstacles for the G-7, G-8, and G-20. It is essential for economists and diplomats to closely monitor and actively engage with these forums to ensure effective global economic governance and sustainable development. Additionally, the implications of these groups on regional economic integration and cooperation cannot be overlooked, as they have the potential to either strengthen or hinder the progress of regional economic blocs.

Prospects and Challenges for the G-7, G-8, and G-20 in a Changing World Economy

In today's rapidly changing global economy, the G-7, G-8, and G-20 have emerged as key players in shaping economic policies and governance. These international forums bring together some of the world's most powerful economies, providing a platform for economists and diplomats to discuss and coordinate on crucial issues. From the economic importance and future of these groups to their impact on trade, globalization, inequality, poverty, financial stability, environmental sustainability, innovation, and regional economic integration, the prospects and challenges for the G-7, G-8, and G-20 are vast and multifaceted.

The G-7, consisting of Canada, France, Germany, Italy, Japan, the United Kingdom, and the United States, has historically played a dominant role in global economic governance. However, as emerging economies gain prominence, the future of the G-7 is being questioned. The rise of regional blocs, such as ASEAN and BRICS, also presents new challenges for the G-7's influence. Nevertheless, the G-7 retains its economic importance as a forum for discussing and coordinating policies on issues ranging from monetary policy to fiscal sustainability.

The G-8, which includes Russia in addition to the G-7 nations, faces similar challenges and opportunities. Russia's inclusion has added geopolitical complexity to the group, raising questions about its future relevance and effectiveness. The G-8's impact on international trade and globalization remains significant, particularly as it addresses issues such as protectionism and market access.

The G-20, comprising the G-8 countries plus emerging economies like China, India, and Brazil, has emerged as a more inclusive forum for global economic governance. It provides a platform for addressing issues of global economic inequality and poverty, as well as promoting financial stability and regulation. The G-20 has also taken on a crucial role in addressing environmental sustainability and its impact on future economic development.

Looking ahead, the G-7, G-8, and G-20 face both potential opportunities and challenges. The rise of emerging economies and regional blocs presents opportunities for greater cooperation and coordination, but also challenges the dominance of traditional powers. Additionally, the COVID-19 pandemic has highlighted the need for the G-7, G-8, and G-20 to address global health crises and pandemics effectively.

Furthermore, these groups have implications for regional economic integration and cooperation. Their policies and decisions can influence regional trade agreements and economic alliances, shaping the future landscape of international commerce.

In conclusion, the G-7, G-8, and G-20 play crucial roles in global economic governance. Their impact on international trade, globalization, inequality, poverty, financial stability, environmental sustainability, innovation, and regional economic integration cannot be understated. As the world economy continues to evolve, these groups must adapt to the changing dynamics, address emerging challenges, and seize new opportunities to ensure a prosperous and sustainable future for all nations.

The Future of G-7, G-8, and G-20 in Light of Emerging Economies and Regional Blocs

In this subchapter, we will explore the future prospects of G-7, G-8, and G-20 in the context of emerging economies and regional blocs. This topic is of utmost importance for economists and diplomats who are keen on understanding the evolving dynamics of global economic governance.

The Economic Importance and The Future of the G-7, G-8, and G-20:

The G-7, G-8, and G-20 have historically played a significant role in shaping global economic policies. However, with the rise of emerging economies such as China, India, and Brazil, there is a need to reassess their relevance and effectiveness. The future of these groups will largely depend on their ability to adapt and include these emerging economies in decision-making processes.

The impact of G-7, G-8, and G-20 on international trade and globalization:

The G-7, G-8, and G-20 have been instrumental in promoting international trade and globalization. However, the emergence of regional blocs like the European Union and the African Union has created new avenues for economic integration. The future of these groups will depend on their ability to collaborate and coordinate with regional blocs to ensure a cohesive and inclusive global trading system.

The role of G-7, G-8, and G-20 in addressing global economic inequality and poverty:

Global economic inequality and poverty remain pressing challenges. The G-7, G-8, and G-20 have a crucial role to play in addressing these issues through inclusive economic policies and targeted initiatives. The future of these groups will depend on their commitment to reducing inequality and alleviating poverty through coordinated efforts.

The influence of G-7, G-8, and G-20 on global financial stability and regulation:

Maintaining global financial stability and effective regulation is crucial for sustained economic growth. The G-7, G-8, and G-20 have been instrumental in coordinating financial policies and regulations. However, with the emergence of new financial centers in Asia and the Middle East, the future of these groups will depend on their ability to adapt and collaborate with these emerging financial powers.

The environmental sustainability agenda of G-7, G-8, and G-20 and its impact on future economic development:

Addressing climate change and promoting sustainable development are key challenges for the global economy. The G-7, G-8, and G-20 have taken steps towards environmental sustainability, but their future will depend on their ability to lead the global transition to a low-carbon economy and foster green innovation.

In conclusion, the future prospects of G-7, G-8, and G-20 are closely tied to the emergence of new economies and regional blocs. These groups must adapt and collaborate with emerging powers, address global challenges, and promote inclusive economic policies to remain relevant and effective in the evolving global economic governance landscape.

Chapter 2: The Impact of G-7, G-8, and G-20 on International Trade and Globalization

The Role of G-7, G-8, and G-20 in Promoting Free Trade and Open Markets

In today's interconnected world, the promotion of free trade and open markets is crucial for global economic growth and development. The G-7, G-8, and G-20 play significant roles in shaping and advancing these principles, ensuring a level playing field for all nations involved. This subchapter will explore the importance of these groups in promoting free trade and open markets, highlighting their impact on international trade and globalization.

The G-7, consisting of the world's leading industrialized nations, has historically been at the forefront of promoting free trade. Through regular summit meetings, member countries discuss economic issues and coordinate policies to eliminate barriers to trade. Their commitment to open markets has resulted in the reduction of tariffs, the removal of trade restrictions, and the facilitation of cross-border investments. The G-7 also serves as a platform to address trade imbalances and resolve disputes, fostering a more cooperative and inclusive global trading system.

Building upon the G-7's efforts, the G-8 expanded its membership to include Russia, recognizing the need for broader representation in global economic governance. However, it is the G-20 that has emerged as the premier forum for international economic cooperation. Comprising the world's major economies, including emerging markets, the G-20 brings together a diverse range of perspectives, ensuring a more inclusive approach to promoting free trade and open markets.

The G-20's influence on international trade and globalization cannot be overstated. Through its commitment to multilateralism, the group has played a pivotal role in advancing the World Trade Organization's agenda and resolving trade disputes. Moreover, the G-20 has been instrumental in coordinating responses to global economic crises, such as the 2008 financial meltdown, by promoting stability and preventing protectionist measures.

By advocating for open markets and free trade, the G-7, G-8, and G-20 have been instrumental in driving global economic growth and reducing poverty. Their efforts have facilitated the integration of developing economies into the global trading system, enabling them to access larger markets and benefit from global supply chains. This has contributed to poverty reduction, improved living standards, and enhanced economic opportunities for millions of people worldwide.

In conclusion, the G-7, G-8, and G-20 have played pivotal roles in promoting free trade and open markets. Through their commitment to multilateralism, these groups have fostered economic cooperation, reduced trade barriers, and ensured a level playing field for all nations. As economists and diplomats, it is crucial to recognize the impact of these groups on international trade and globalization and continue supporting their efforts to create a more prosperous and inclusive global economy.

The Influence of G-7, G-8, and G-20 on Global Trade Agreements

Global trade agreements play a crucial role in shaping the economic landscape of nations and promoting international cooperation. Within this context, the G-7, G-8, and G-20 have emerged as key players in influencing and advancing global trade agreements. This subchapter will explore the significant influence of these economic forums on international trade and globalization.

The G-7, G-8, and G-20 have been instrumental in promoting free trade and reducing barriers to economic exchange among member countries. Through regular summits, these forums provide a platform for economists and diplomats to discuss and negotiate trade policies that facilitate economic growth and foster cooperation. By bringing together the world's leading economies, they have the influence to shape global trade agreements, setting the tone for trade relations worldwide.

One notable example of the impact of the G-7, G-8, and G-20 on global trade agreements is the promotion of multilateral trade negotiations. These forums have actively supported initiatives such as the World Trade Organization (WTO) and have encouraged member countries to engage in trade liberalization efforts. By fostering dialogue and consensus-building, they have played a pivotal role in advancing global trade agreements, including the establishment of the WTO's Doha Round.

Furthermore, the G-7, G-8, and G-20 have addressed issues related to trade imbalances and unfair trade practices. Through discussions and negotiations, they have sought to create a level playing field for international trade, ensuring that rules and regulations are fair and transparent. By addressing these concerns, they have helped to reduce trade tensions and promote a more stable and predictable global trading system.

In recent years, the G-7, G-8, and G-20 have also recognized the importance of digital trade and e-commerce. They have emphasized the need to adapt trade agreements to the digital age, recognizing its potential to drive economic growth and innovation. By addressing barriers to digital trade and promoting digital connectivity, these forums have contributed to the expansion of global trade in the digital economy.

In conclusion, the G-7, G-8, and G-20 have exerted significant influence on global trade agreements. Through their discussions, negotiations, and policy recommendations, they have shaped the direction of international trade and promoted economic cooperation among nations. As economists and diplomats, understanding the role of these forums in influencing global trade agreements is crucial for navigating the complex landscape of international trade and promoting economic growth.

The Effects of G-7, G-8, and G-20 on Globalization and Economic Integration

The G-7, G-8, and G-20 have played a significant role in shaping global economic governance and have had profound effects on globalization and economic integration. This subchapter explores the various ways in which these international forums have impacted the global economy and their implications for the future.

Firstly, the G-7, G-8, and G-20 have been instrumental in promoting international trade and globalization. These forums have facilitated dialogue and cooperation among the world's largest economies, leading to the reduction of trade barriers and the promotion of free trade. This has resulted in increased economic integration and boosted global economic growth.

Furthermore, the G-7, G-8, and G-20 have recognized the importance of addressing global economic inequality and poverty. Through various initiatives and policy discussions, these forums have aimed to reduce poverty and promote inclusive economic growth. They have recognized that economic integration should benefit all segments of society and have worked towards creating a more equitable global economic system.

In addition, the G-7, G-8, and G-20 have played a crucial role in ensuring global financial stability and regulation. These forums have been at the forefront of coordinating global responses to financial crises, strengthening financial regulations, and promoting stability in the global financial system. Their efforts have helped prevent and mitigate financial crises, ensuring the stability of the global economy.

Another area where the G-7, G-8, and G-20 have made significant contributions is in addressing environmental sustainability. Recognizing the importance of sustainable development, these forums have placed environmental issues high on their agenda. They have worked towards promoting green growth, reducing carbon emissions, and fostering international cooperation on climate change. Their efforts have had a profound impact on future economic development and have paved the way for a more sustainable and environmentally conscious global economy.

Moreover, the G-7, G-8, and G-20 have played a crucial role in shaping global economic policies and governance. These forums have provided a platform for policymakers to discuss and coordinate their economic policies, leading to greater policy coherence and harmonization. Their influence on global economic policies has been substantial, and they have contributed to the establishment of international norms and standards.

Looking ahead, the future prospects of the G-7, G-8, and G-20 are influenced by emerging economies and regional blocs. As the global economic landscape continues to evolve, these forums will need to adapt and engage with emerging economies to maintain their relevance and effectiveness.

However, the G-7, G-8, and G-20 also face potential challenges and opportunities in a post-pandemic world. The COVID-19 pandemic has exposed vulnerabilities in the global economy and highlighted the need for greater international cooperation. These forums will play a critical role in addressing the economic and health challenges posed by pandemics and in promoting global recovery and resilience.

Furthermore, the G-7, G-8, and G-20 have implications for regional economic integration and cooperation. Their efforts to promote global economic integration can also have spill-over effects on regional economic blocs, fostering greater cooperation and integration at the regional level.

In conclusion, the G-7, G-8, and G-20 have had significant effects on globalization and economic integration. From promoting international trade and addressing global economic inequality, to ensuring financial stability and environmental sustainability, these forums have played a vital role in shaping the global economic landscape. As the world continues to evolve, the G-7, G-8, and G-20 will face new opportunities and challenges in their quest to foster global economic governance and cooperation.

The Challenges and Opportunities for G-7, G-8, and G-20 in a Rapidly Changing Global Trade Landscape

In today's rapidly changing global trade landscape, the G-7, G-8, and G-20 face both challenges and opportunities in their pursuit of global economic governance. Economists and diplomats play a crucial role in understanding and addressing these issues, as they strive to ensure economic stability, promote sustainable development, and address global economic inequalities.

One of the key challenges faced by the G-7, G-8, and G-20 is the economic importance and future of these groups. With emerging economies and regional blocs gaining prominence, there is a need for the G-7, G-8, and G-20 to adapt and evolve to remain relevant in the changing economic landscape. This requires fostering dialogue and cooperation with these emerging economies while maintaining their leadership roles.

Another challenge lies in the impact of the G-7, G-8, and G-20 on international trade and globalization. As the world becomes increasingly interconnected, these groups must navigate trade tensions, protectionism, and the rise of nationalist policies. Finding common ground and promoting free and fair trade is crucial for global economic growth and stability.

Addressing global economic inequality and poverty is another significant challenge for the G-7, G-8, and G-20. These groups must work towards creating inclusive economic policies, promoting social development, and reducing poverty levels. By fostering economic opportunities and providing aid to developing countries, they can play a vital role in reducing global inequality.

Furthermore, the G-7, G-8, and G-20 have a responsibility to ensure global financial stability and regulation. They must strengthen international financial institutions, enhance regulatory frameworks, and promote transparency in the global financial system. By doing so, they can mitigate financial crises and promote stability in the global economy.

The environmental sustainability agenda is another crucial area where the G-7, G-8, and G-20 can make a significant impact. These groups must prioritize sustainable development, combat climate change, and promote clean energy initiatives. By aligning their efforts, they can drive future economic development while preserving the planet for future generations.

The G-7, G-8, and G-20 also play a critical role in shaping global economic policies and governance. Their decisions and recommendations have far-reaching implications for global trade, investment, and economic cooperation. Economists and diplomats must actively engage in these processes to ensure that policies are evidence-based, inclusive, and promote the common good.

Moreover, the G-7, G-8, and G-20 are instrumental in promoting innovation and technological advancements. They must foster an environment that encourages research and development, supports entrepreneurship, and promotes digitalization. By embracing innovation, they can drive economic growth and enhance the competitiveness of their member countries.

Looking towards the future, the G-7, G-8, and G-20 face both challenges and opportunities in light of emerging economies and regional blocs. They must adapt their structures and decision-making processes to reflect the changing economic dynamics. By embracing diversity and inclusivity, they can foster cooperation and address global challenges more effectively.

In a post-pandemic world, the G-7, G-8, and G-20 will encounter new challenges and opportunities. They must play a crucial role in rebuilding economies, supporting recovery efforts, and strengthening global health systems. Economists and diplomats must collaborate to ensure that these groups effectively respond to future health crises and pandemics.

Lastly, the implications of the G-7, G-8, and G-20 on regional economic integration and cooperation cannot be overlooked. These groups have the potential to promote regional economic integration, enhance cooperation, and strengthen regional blocs. By fostering dialogue and collaboration, they can contribute to regional stability and economic growth.

In conclusion, the challenges and opportunities for the G-7, G-8, and G-20 in a rapidly changing global trade landscape require the active engagement of economists and diplomats. By addressing economic importance, trade, inequality, financial stability, sustainability, innovation, and future prospects, these groups can shape global economic policies and governance. The potential challenges and opportunities in a post-pandemic world and their role in addressing global health crises and regional economic integration are also crucial considerations. As economists and diplomats, it is imperative to understand and navigate these complexities to ensure a prosperous and inclusive global economic future.

Chapter 3: The Role of G-7, G-8, and G-20 in Addressing Global Economic Inequality and Poverty

The Efforts of G-7, G-8, and G-20 in Reducing Income Disparities

Income disparities have long been a pressing issue in global economic governance, and the G-7, G-8, and G-20 have recognized the importance of addressing this issue to promote global economic stability and sustainable development. These influential international forums have taken various initiatives to reduce income disparities and alleviate poverty on a global scale.

One of the key strategies employed by the G-7, G-8, and G-20 is promoting inclusive economic growth. Recognizing that economic growth alone is not sufficient to address income disparities, these forums have emphasized the need for growth to benefit all segments of society. Policies and measures have been put in place to ensure that the benefits of economic growth are distributed more equitably, particularly to the most vulnerable populations.

Another important aspect of the efforts to reduce income disparities is the focus on social protection and safety nets. The G-7, G-8, and G-20 have recognized that a well-functioning social protection system is crucial to mitigating the negative impacts of income disparities. These forums have encouraged member countries to invest in social safety nets, such as unemployment benefits, healthcare, and education, to provide a safety net for the most vulnerable individuals and families.

Furthermore, the G-7, G-8, and G-20 have emphasized the importance of enhancing access to quality education and healthcare. Recognizing that education and healthcare are fundamental to reducing income disparities, these forums have called for increased investment in these sectors. Efforts have been made to improve access to education and healthcare services, particularly for marginalized populations, to ensure that everyone has equal opportunities to succeed and thrive.

Additionally, the G-7, G-8, and G-20 have recognized the importance of addressing gender inequalities in income distribution. These forums have advocated for policies and measures to promote gender equality in the workforce and reduce the gender pay gap. Efforts have been made to empower women economically and ensure their equal participation in decision-making processes.

While progress has been made in reducing income disparities, challenges remain. The G-7, G-8, and G-20 continue to work towards finding innovative solutions to address income disparities and promote inclusive growth. Collaboration among member countries, as well as engagement with international organizations and civil society, is crucial in achieving meaningful results.

In conclusion, the G-7, G-8, and G-20 have made significant efforts to reduce income disparities and promote inclusive economic growth. Through various strategies, such as promoting inclusive growth, investing in social protection, enhancing access to education and healthcare, and addressing gender inequalities, these forums have made strides in reducing income disparities and alleviating poverty. However, continued collaboration and innovation are necessary to overcome the challenges and ensure that the benefits of economic growth are shared by all.

The Impact of G-7, G-8, and G-20 on Poverty Alleviation Programs

In the realm of global economic governance, the G-7, G-8, and G-20 have played significant roles in addressing various global challenges, including poverty alleviation. These groups, consisting of the world's most powerful economies, have the potential to shape policies and initiatives that can have a profound impact on poverty reduction efforts worldwide.

The G-7, originally established as an informal forum for economic cooperation among the world's leading industrialized nations, expanded to become the G-8 with the inclusion of Russia in 1998. More recently, the G-20 emerged as a more inclusive platform, bringing together both developed and developing economies. While the G-7 and G-8 have traditionally focused on economic and financial issues, the G-20 has taken a broader approach, encompassing a range of economic and social concerns.

One of the key areas where these groups have made a significant impact is in poverty alleviation programs. Through their collective efforts, they have been able to mobilize resources, promote cooperation, and implement policies that aim to reduce poverty levels globally. These initiatives have included increased foreign aid, debt relief for developing countries, and support for sustainable development projects.

One notable example of the G-7, G-8, and G-20's impact on poverty alleviation is the commitment to achieving the United Nations' Millennium Development Goals (MDGs). These goals, which included targets for poverty reduction, were endorsed by these groups and served as a guiding framework for their actions. While progress has been made in many areas, challenges remain, particularly in regions with high levels of poverty and inequality.

Furthermore, the G-7, G-8, and G-20 have recognized the importance of promoting inclusive growth as a means of tackling poverty. They have emphasized the need for policies that ensure equitable distribution of wealth and opportunities, as well as investments in education, healthcare, and social protection. Moreover, they have acknowledged the role of entrepreneurship and innovation in poverty reduction and have sought to create an enabling environment for these activities.

Despite these efforts, critics argue that the impact of the G-7, G-8, and G-20 on poverty alleviation programs has been limited. They highlight the challenges of implementing policies across diverse economies and the need for greater accountability and transparency in decision-making processes. Additionally, the emergence of regional blocs and the rise of emerging economies have presented new challenges and opportunities that these groups must address.

In conclusion, while the G-7, G-8, and G-20 have made significant contributions to poverty alleviation programs, there is still much work to be done. These groups must continue to prioritize poverty reduction and address the structural issues that perpetuate inequality. As the world faces new challenges, such as the post-pandemic recovery and the need for sustainable development, the G-7, G-8, and G-20 must adapt and evolve to ensure their continued relevance and effectiveness in addressing global poverty.

G-7, G-8, and G-20 Initiatives for Sustainable Development and Inclusive Growth

The G-7, G-8, and G-20 have been at the forefront of global economic governance, playing a pivotal role in shaping policies and addressing key challenges. These groups have made significant efforts to promote sustainable development and inclusive growth, recognizing their economic importance and impact on various aspects of the global economy.

One of the key areas where the G-7, G-8, and G-20 have focused their initiatives is in addressing global economic inequality and poverty. These groups have recognized the importance of reducing income disparities and ensuring that the benefits of economic growth are shared more equitably. Through various initiatives, such as promoting inclusive financial systems and social safety nets, they have worked towards creating a more inclusive and fair global economy.

Moreover, the G-7, G-8, and G-20 have played a crucial role in promoting environmental sustainability. Recognizing the urgent need to tackle climate change and preserve the planet for future generations, these groups have taken initiatives to promote clean energy, reduce greenhouse gas emissions, and foster sustainable development practices. By setting ambitious targets and encouraging international cooperation, they have been instrumental in driving the global sustainability agenda.

In addition to their focus on inequality and the environment, the G-7, G-8, and G-20 have also played a pivotal role in ensuring global financial stability and regulation. Through coordinated efforts, they have strengthened financial regulations, enhanced transparency, and promoted responsible financial practices. Their actions have been crucial in preventing future financial crises and maintaining stability in the global financial system.

Furthermore, these groups have recognized the importance of innovation and technological advancements in driving economic growth. By fostering an environment conducive to research and development, promoting entrepreneurship, and encouraging investment in emerging technologies, they have played a key role in promoting innovation and technological advancements.

Looking towards the future, the G-7, G-8, and G-20 face both challenges and opportunities. With the emergence of new economies and regional blocs, there is a need for these groups to adapt and evolve to remain relevant. Additionally, the ongoing COVID-19 pandemic has highlighted the importance of global cooperation in addressing health crises, and the G-7, G-8, and G-20 have a crucial role to play in this regard.

In conclusion, the G-7, G-8, and G-20 have been instrumental in promoting sustainable development and inclusive growth. Through their initiatives, they have addressed economic inequality, promoted environmental sustainability, ensured financial stability, and fostered innovation. As the global economic landscape evolves, these groups will need to adapt and seize opportunities while working together to overcome challenges and shape a more prosperous and equitable future.

Challenges Faced by G-7, G-8, and G-20 in Addressing Global Economic Inequality and Poverty

In the pursuit of global economic governance, G-7, G-8, and G-20 have played significant roles in shaping policies and addressing various global challenges. However, one of the most pressing issues that continue to persist is the problem of global economic inequality and poverty. Despite their efforts, these groups face numerous challenges in effectively addressing this issue.

Firstly, the sheer complexity and magnitude of global economic inequality and poverty pose a significant challenge. The G-7, G-8, and G-20 have to navigate through diverse economic systems, varying levels of development, and contrasting policy priorities among member countries. This diversity makes it difficult to develop consensus and implement effective strategies to reduce inequality and poverty on a global scale.

Secondly, the influence of powerful interest groups and vested economic interests can hinder progress in addressing global economic inequality. Wealthy nations and influential corporations often prioritize their own economic growth and profit, making it challenging to implement policies that address poverty and inequality. This poses a significant obstacle for G-7, G-8, and G-20 in effectively addressing these issues.

Additionally, the lack of a comprehensive and coordinated approach to tackling global economic inequality and poverty is a significant challenge. While individual member countries may have their own initiatives, the absence of a unified strategy can lead to fragmented efforts and limited impact. G-7, G-8, and G-20 must work towards developing a holistic approach that encompasses various dimensions of inequality and poverty, including income disparities, access to education and healthcare, and social protection.

Moreover, the influence of emerging economies and regional blocs presents both challenges and opportunities. As these economies gain prominence, they bring new perspectives and priorities to the table. G-7, G-8, and G-20 must navigate these dynamics and ensure inclusive decision-making processes that address the concerns and needs of both established and emerging economies.

Lastly, the COVID-19 pandemic has exacerbated global economic inequality and poverty, posing additional challenges for G-7, G-8, and G-20. The pandemic has disrupted economies, increased unemployment rates, and pushed more people into poverty. G-7, G-8, and G-20 must respond with coordinated efforts to mitigate the impact of the pandemic on vulnerable populations and ensure a sustainable and equitable recovery.

In conclusion, G-7, G-8, and G-20 face significant challenges in addressing global economic inequality and poverty. The complexity of the issue, the influence of vested interests, the lack of a comprehensive approach, the rise of emerging economies, and the impact of the COVID-19 pandemic all contribute to the difficulties faced by these groups. Nonetheless, with concerted efforts, inclusive decision-making, and a coordinated approach, G-7, G-8, and G-20 can play a crucial role in reducing global economic inequality and poverty, ultimately fostering a more equitable and prosperous world.

Chapter 4: The Influence of G-7, G-8, and G-20 on Global Financial Stability and Regulation

The Role of G-7, G-8, and G-20 in Financial Crisis Management

In times of financial crisis, the G-7, G-8, and G-20 play a crucial role in managing and stabilizing global economies. As economists and diplomats are well aware, these international economic forums have evolved over the years to address various challenges faced by the global community. One of their key responsibilities is to ensure financial stability and regulation on a global scale.

The G-7, initially established in 1975, consists of the world's most advanced economies, including the United States, Japan, Germany, France, the United Kingdom, Italy, and Canada. It serves as an informal platform for these countries to discuss economic policies and coordinate their actions to address financial crises. However, with the changing dynamics of the global economy, the G-8 was formed in 1997 to include Russia. This expansion aimed to incorporate emerging economies into the discussions.

The G-20, established in 1999, further broadened the scope of global economic governance by including developing countries and regional blocs. This move acknowledged the importance of their contributions to the global economy and recognized that their involvement was crucial in managing financial crises effectively.

During times of financial turmoil, the G-7, G-8, and G-20 play a critical role in coordinating policies, sharing information, and implementing measures to restore stability. Through their collective efforts, these forums facilitate dialogue among nations, enabling them to identify and address systemic risks to financial markets. They work towards developing effective regulatory frameworks, promoting transparency, and enhancing cooperation between countries.

Furthermore, the G-7, G-8, and G-20 also play a significant role in providing financial assistance to countries in need during a crisis. They establish mechanisms such as loan facilities, debt relief programs, and emergency funding to stabilize economies and prevent the spread of financial contagion.

In recent years, the G-7, G-8, and G-20 have faced numerous challenges, including the 2008 global financial crisis, the Eurozone debt crisis, and the ongoing COVID-19 pandemic. These crises have highlighted the importance of strong global economic governance and the need for effective coordination among nations.

Looking ahead, the role of the G-7, G-8, and G-20 in financial crisis management remains crucial. As emerging economies and regional blocs gain prominence, there is a need for continued engagement and collaboration between advanced and developing nations. By working together, these forums can ensure a stable and resilient global financial system that promotes economic growth and reduces inequality.

The Impact of G-7, G-8, and G-20 on Global Financial Regulations

Introduction:

In today's interconnected global economy, financial regulations play a crucial role in maintaining stability and ensuring fair competition. The G-7, G-8, and G-20, as influential international forums, have had a significant impact on shaping global financial regulations. This subchapter examines the role of these groups in establishing and enforcing regulations, their impact on global financial stability, and the challenges they face in a rapidly changing economic landscape.

The Influence of G-7, G-8, and G-20:

The G-7, G-8, and G-20 have been instrumental in shaping global financial regulations. Through their collective actions, these groups have played a vital role in standardizing regulatory frameworks, enhancing transparency, and promoting cooperation among nations. They have established international bodies such as the Financial Stability Board (FSB) and the Basel Committee on Banking Supervision (BCBS), which have been crucial in setting global standards for financial regulation.

Impact on Global Financial Stability and Regulation:

The G-7, G-8, and G-20 have made significant strides in promoting global financial stability and regulation. They have worked towards strengthening oversight of financial institutions, improving risk management practices, and enhancing regulatory coordination across borders. The implementation of regulatory measures such as Basel III has helped to prevent a recurrence of the 2008 financial crisis and has increased the resilience of the global financial system.

Challenges and Opportunities:

However, the G-7, G-8, and G-20 face various challenges in their efforts to regulate global finance effectively. One major challenge is the rapid evolution of financial technology (fintech) and the emergence of cryptocurrencies, which require innovative regulatory approaches. Additionally, the rise of emerging economies and regional blocs has necessitated greater inclusivity and representation in global financial regulation discussions.

Conclusion:

The G-7, G-8, and G-20 have played a crucial role in shaping global financial regulations. Through their collective efforts, they have enhanced global financial stability and laid the groundwork for fair and transparent financial systems. However, they face ongoing challenges in adapting to a rapidly changing economic landscape, including the need to address emerging technologies and accommodate the rising influence of emerging economies. By recognizing these challenges and opportunities, the G-7, G-8, and G-20 can continue to shape global financial regulations effectively and promote a more stable and inclusive global economy. Economists and diplomats must actively engage with these groups to ensure that financial regulations evolve to meet the needs of an interconnected world.

G-7, G-8, and G-20 Initiatives to Enhance Financial Stability and Risk Mitigation

In the ever-changing landscape of global economic governance, the G-7, G-8, and G-20 have played a crucial role in enhancing financial stability and mitigating risks. These initiatives have been instrumental in addressing the challenges posed by economic inequality, poverty, globalization, and financial instability. Economists and diplomats have recognized the significance of these forums in shaping global economic policies and governance.

One of the key contributions of the G-7, G-8, and G-20 has been their efforts to promote financial stability and regulation. These forums have recognized the importance of robust financial systems in ensuring sustainable economic growth. They have implemented various measures to strengthen financial institutions, enhance market transparency, and promote responsible lending practices. By coordinating their actions, these forums have been able to mitigate the risks posed by global financial crises and prevent them from escalating into systemic failures.

Furthermore, the G-7, G-8, and G-20 have also focused on enhancing risk mitigation strategies. They have recognized the interconnectedness of global markets and the need for coordinated risk management. Through initiatives such as stress tests, regulatory frameworks, and information sharing, these forums have worked towards identifying potential vulnerabilities and developing mechanisms to address them.

By collaborating with international financial institutions and regulatory bodies, they have been able to establish a more resilient and stable financial system.

In addition to financial stability, the G-7, G-8, and G-20 have also prioritized the environmental sustainability agenda. They have recognized the urgent need to address climate change and promote sustainable development. Through initiatives such as the Paris Agreement and the Green Climate Fund, these forums have committed to reducing greenhouse gas emissions, supporting clean energy technologies, and mobilizing financial resources for climate action. By integrating sustainability into their economic policies, they have aimed to ensure a greener and more inclusive future.

Looking ahead, the future prospects of the G-7, G-8, and G-20 are influenced by emerging economies and regional blocs. As the global economic landscape continues to evolve, these forums will need to adapt and engage with new actors. They will also face challenges and opportunities in a post-pandemic world, including the need to address health crises and support global recovery.

In conclusion, the G-7, G-8, and G-20 have played a pivotal role in enhancing financial stability and risk mitigation. These forums have implemented various initiatives to strengthen financial systems and promote responsible lending practices. They have also recognized the importance of environmental sustainability and have committed to addressing climate change. As the global economic governance landscape continues to evolve, the G-7, G-8, and G-20 will need to adapt and collaborate with emerging economies and regional blocs to address future challenges and opportunities. Their role in shaping global economic policies and governance remains crucial in promoting innovation, technological advancements, and regional economic integration.

Challenges and Controversies Surrounding G-7, G-8, and G-20 in Financial Governance

As global economic governance institutions, the G-7, G-8, and G-20 have played a crucial role in shaping the international economic landscape and addressing various global challenges. However, these forums have also faced numerous challenges and controversies in their pursuit of financial governance. This subchapter will delve into the key issues surrounding the G-7, G-8, and G-20, and analyze their impact on different aspects of the global economy.

One of the major debates is centered around the economic importance and future prospects of the G-7, G-8, and G-20. Critics argue that these forums are not representative of the changing global economic order, as emerging economies and regional blocs gain increasing prominence. They question the legitimacy and effectiveness of these institutions in addressing the needs and concerns of all nations.

Moreover, the impact of the G-7, G-8, and G-20 on international trade and globalization has been a subject of contention. While some praise their efforts in promoting free trade and economic integration, others criticize them for perpetuating global economic inequality and favoring developed nations. The role of these forums in addressing global economic inequality and poverty will be explored, shedding light on their successes and limitations in achieving inclusive growth.

Financial stability and regulation are crucial for sustainable economic development. The G-7, G-8, and G-20 have been at the forefront of discussions on global financial stability, aiming to prevent future financial crises. However, challenges arise in reconciling the interests of diverse economies and regulating complex financial systems. The subchapter will examine the controversies surrounding their regulatory efforts and explore potential solutions.

Another pressing issue is the environmental sustainability agenda of the G-7, G-8, and G-20 and its impact on future economic development. Critics argue that these forums have not done enough to address environmental challenges and promote sustainable growth. The subchapter will analyze the influence and effectiveness of their environmental policies and explore the potential for greater collaboration in achieving global sustainability goals.

Furthermore, the subchapter will delve into the role of the G-7, G-8, and G-20 in shaping global economic policies and governance. It will discuss their influence on regional economic integration and cooperation and the potential implications for developing economies. The subchapter will also examine the importance of these forums in promoting innovation and technological advancements, as well as their potential challenges and opportunities in a post-pandemic world.

Lastly, the subchapter will explore the role of the G-7, G-8, and G-20 in addressing global health crises and pandemics. The COVID-19 pandemic has highlighted the need for international cooperation in health emergencies, and the effectiveness of these forums in responding to such crises will be analyzed.

In conclusion, the challenges and controversies surrounding the G-7, G-8, and G-20 in financial governance are multifaceted and require careful analysis. Economists and diplomats must critically assess the impact of these forums on various aspects of the global economy, ranging from trade and poverty to financial stability and the environment. By addressing these challenges and controversies, we can pave the way for more effective and inclusive global economic governance.

Chapter 5: The Environmental Sustainability Agenda of G-7, G-8, and G-20 and Its Impact on Future Economic Development

G-7, G-8, and G-20's Efforts in Combating Climate Change and Promoting Clean Energy

In recent years, the global community has witnessed an increasing recognition of the urgent need to address climate change and transition towards a sustainable and clean energy future. As key global economic forums, the G-7, G-8, and G-20 have played a crucial role in shaping the environmental sustainability agenda and promoting clean energy initiatives.

The G-7, consisting of the world's most advanced economies, has been at the forefront of efforts to combat climate change and promote clean energy. Through various declarations and commitments, the G-7 has emphasized the importance of reducing greenhouse gas emissions, transitioning to renewable energy sources, and fostering international cooperation in addressing climate-related challenges. The G-7 has also supported initiatives to promote energy efficiency, sustainable agriculture, and biodiversity conservation.

Building upon the G-7's efforts, the G-8 expanded the focus on climate change and clean energy to include emerging economies such as Russia, China, India, and Brazil. The G-8 has sought to foster dialogue and collaboration between developed and developing countries, recognizing that a global response to climate change requires the participation of all nations. Through initiatives such as the Gleneagles Dialogue and the Major Economies Forum, the G-8 has facilitated discussions on climate change mitigation, adaptation, and technology transfer.

With the emergence of the G-20 as the premier forum for international economic cooperation, the global response to climate change has gained further momentum. The G-20 has recognized the close linkages between climate change and economic development, emphasizing the need for sustainable and low-carbon growth strategies. The G-20 has also focused on mobilizing financial resources for climate action, promoting green finance, and encouraging the private sector's engagement in clean energy investments.

While the G-7, G-8, and G-20 have made significant strides in combating climate change and promoting clean energy, challenges remain. The transition to a sustainable and clean energy future requires substantial investments, technology transfers, and policy coordination among nations. The forums must continue to prioritize climate-related issues and ensure that their commitments translate into concrete actions at the national and international levels.

In conclusion, the G-7, G-8, and G-20 have played a pivotal role in promoting global efforts to combat climate change and transition towards a sustainable and clean energy future. Through their declarations, commitments, and initiatives, these forums have fostered international cooperation, mobilized financial resources, and encouraged the adoption of environmentally friendly policies. However, the road ahead is challenging, and continued efforts are needed to address climate change effectively and achieve a sustainable future for all.

The Role of G-7, G-8, and G-20 in Sustainable Development and Green Finance

In recent years, the global community has witnessed an increasing focus on sustainable development and the urgent need to address environmental challenges. As key players in global economic governance, the G-7, G-8, and G-20 have recognized the importance of integrating sustainability into their agendas and have taken significant steps towards promoting sustainable development and green finance.

Sustainable development requires a comprehensive approach that encompasses economic, social, and environmental dimensions. The G-7, G-8, and G-20 have acknowledged this and have made commitments to support sustainable development goals and initiatives. They have recognized that sustainable development is not only crucial for the future of our planet but also for long-term economic prosperity.

One of the key ways in which the G-7, G-8, and G-20 have contributed to sustainable development is through their efforts to promote green finance. Green finance refers to the financing of projects that have a positive impact on the environment and contribute to sustainable development. The G-7, G-8, and G-20 have played a crucial role in mobilizing private sector investments towards sustainable projects and encouraging financial institutions to integrate environmental considerations into their decision-making processes.

Moreover, the G-7, G-8, and G-20 have also focused on addressing climate change and reducing greenhouse gas emissions. They have recognized the importance of transitioning to a low-carbon economy and have committed to supporting clean energy initiatives, promoting renewable energy sources, and encouraging the adoption of sustainable practices in various sectors.

In addition to their efforts in green finance and climate change, the G-7, G-8, and G-20 have also played a significant role in addressing other environmental challenges such as biodiversity loss, deforestation, and pollution. They have advocated for the preservation of natural resources, the protection of ecosystems, and the promotion of sustainable land and water management practices.

By integrating sustainability into their agendas, the G-7, G-8, and G-20 have not only contributed to a more environmentally conscious global economy but also to future economic development. They have recognized that sustainable development and economic growth are not mutually exclusive but rather interconnected, and that addressing environmental challenges is essential for long-term economic stability and prosperity.

In conclusion, the G-7, G-8, and G-20 have played a crucial role in promoting sustainable development and green finance. Their efforts in integrating sustainability into their agendas, promoting green finance, and addressing environmental challenges have not only contributed to the global sustainability agenda but also to future economic development. As economists and diplomats, it is imperative for us to recognize the importance of their role and continue to support their efforts in shaping a sustainable and prosperous future.

The Effects of G-7, G-8, and G-20 Environmental Policies on Economic Growth

In recent decades, there has been an increasing recognition of the impact of environmental issues on economic growth and development. The G-7, G-8, and G-20, as key international economic forums, have played a crucial role in addressing these concerns and shaping environmental policies. This subchapter explores the effects of G-7, G-8, and G-20 environmental policies on economic growth, highlighting the importance of sustainable development and the need for global cooperation.

Environmental sustainability has become a central agenda for the G-7, G-8, and G-20, recognizing that economic growth cannot be achieved at the expense of the environment. These forums have adopted various measures to promote sustainable development, such as reducing greenhouse gas emissions, promoting renewable energy sources, and preserving biodiversity. These policies aim to mitigate the adverse effects of climate change, protect natural resources, and ensure the long-term viability of economic activities.

The implementation of these environmental policies has had both direct and indirect effects on economic growth. Directly, the promotion of clean technologies and renewable energy sources has led to the emergence of new industries and job opportunities. This has stimulated economic growth, particularly in sectors such as renewable energy, energy efficiency, and environmental services. Moreover, the transition to a low-carbon economy has the potential to enhance energy security, reduce dependence on fossil fuels, and lower energy costs in the long run.

Indirectly, the environmental policies of the G-7, G-8, and G-20 have contributed to creating a more sustainable and resilient economic system. By addressing environmental challenges, such as climate change and resource depletion, these policies help mitigate risks and uncertainties that can undermine economic stability and growth. Furthermore, they foster innovation and technological advancements, as businesses and industries are compelled to develop more sustainable practices and technologies.

However, it is important to acknowledge that the implementation of environmental policies can also pose challenges to economic growth, particularly in the short term. For instance, industries heavily reliant on fossil fuels may face transitional difficulties and job losses. Thus, a careful and well-planned approach is necessary to ensure a just and inclusive transition to a sustainable economy.

In conclusion, the environmental sustainability agenda of the G-7, G-8, and G-20 has significant implications for economic growth and development. By promoting sustainable practices and technologies, these forums contribute to economic resilience, job creation, and innovation. However, careful consideration must be given to the potential short-term challenges and the need for inclusive policies that ensure a smooth transition. Ultimately, the integration of environmental concerns into economic policies is crucial for a sustainable and prosperous future.

Challenges and Opportunities for G-7, G-8, and G-20 in Balancing Environmental Concerns and Economic Development

In recent years, there has been a growing recognition of the need to address environmental concerns while promoting economic development. The G-7, G-8, and G-20 have a unique role to play in this regard, as they are influential platforms for global economic governance. This subchapter will discuss the challenges and opportunities that these forums face in striking a balance between environmental concerns and economic development.

One of the key challenges for the G-7, G-8, and G-20 is the tension between economic growth and environmental sustainability. While economic development is essential for lifting people out of poverty and improving living standards, it often comes at the expense of the environment. Finding ways to promote sustainable economic growth that minimizes environmental degradation is a complex task that requires coordinated efforts among member countries.

Moreover, the G-7, G-8, and G-20 face the challenge of aligning their environmental agendas with the diverse interests and priorities of member countries. Different countries have different levels of economic development, resource endowments, and environmental challenges. Balancing these diverse interests and priorities is crucial for the effectiveness and legitimacy of these forums.

However, there are also significant opportunities for the G-7, G-8, and G-20 to address environmental concerns while promoting economic development. These forums can serve as platforms for sharing best practices, promoting technological innovation, and fostering international cooperation on environmental issues. By exchanging knowledge and experiences, member countries can learn from each other and develop more effective policies and strategies.

Additionally, the G-7, G-8, and G-20 can leverage their economic influence to incentivize environmentally friendly practices and investments. By integrating environmental considerations into trade agreements, investment frameworks, and financial regulations, these forums can encourage businesses and investors to adopt sustainable practices and technologies.

Furthermore, the G-7, G-8, and G-20 can play a crucial role in mobilizing financial resources for environmental initiatives. By coordinating efforts to mobilize public and private finance, these forums can support developing countries in their transition to low-carbon and resource-efficient economies.

In conclusion, the G-7, G-8, and G-20 face significant challenges in balancing environmental concerns and economic development. However, there are also ample opportunities for these forums to promote sustainable economic growth and environmental sustainability. By addressing these challenges and seizing these opportunities, the G-7, G-8, and G-20 can contribute to a more sustainable and inclusive global economy.

Chapter 6: The Role of G-7, G-8, and G-20 in Shaping Global Economic Policies and Governance

G-7, G-8, and G-20's Influence on International Economic Institutions

The Global Economic Governance: The Role of G-7, G-8, and G-20 offers a comprehensive analysis of the impact and influence of these prominent international forums on various aspects of global economic governance. This subchapter will delve into the significant influence of G-7, G-8, and G-20 on international economic institutions, addressing the interests of economists and diplomats alike.

Firstly, the Economic Importance and the Future of G-7, G-8, and G-20 will be explored, highlighting their role as key platforms for economic cooperation and decision-making. These forums serve as crucial arenas where policymakers can discuss and coordinate policies to address pressing global economic challenges.

One of the key contributions of G-7, G-8, and G-20 lies in their impact on international trade and globalization. These forums have played a pivotal role in shaping trade agreements, promoting multilateralism, and advancing global economic integration. The subchapter will analyze the specific initiatives and policies undertaken by these forums to facilitate trade liberalization and mitigate protectionist tendencies.

Another important aspect to explore is the role of G-7, G-8, and G-20 in addressing global economic inequality and poverty. These forums have sought to tackle these issues through various mechanisms, including development assistance, poverty reduction programs, and initiatives aimed at promoting inclusive growth. The subchapter will examine the effectiveness of these efforts and highlight potential areas for improvement.

Furthermore, the influence of G-7, G-8, and G-20 on global financial stability and regulation will be discussed. These forums have played a crucial role in shaping international financial architecture, coordinating regulatory frameworks, and responding to financial crises. The subchapter will assess the impact of their initiatives on financial stability and explore avenues for further strengthening global financial governance.

The environmental sustainability agenda of G-7, G-8, and G-20 will also be analyzed, emphasizing its impact on future economic development. These forums have increasingly recognized the importance of sustainable development and have taken measures to address environmental challenges. The subchapter will explore the specific policies and initiatives undertaken by these forums and evaluate their potential implications for economic growth and environmental protection.

Lastly, the subchapter will discuss the role of G-7, G-8, and G-20 in shaping global economic policies and governance, promoting innovation and technological advancements, and addressing global health crises and pandemics. It will also address the potential challenges and opportunities for these forums in a post-pandemic world, as well as their implications on regional economic integration and cooperation.

Overall, this subchapter will provide economists and diplomats with a comprehensive understanding of how G-7, G-8, and G-20 have influenced international economic institutions and shaped global economic governance. It will shed light on the future prospects and challenges faced by these forums in an ever-changing global landscape.

G-7, G-8, and G-20's Role in Crisis Management and Global Economic Coordination

In today's interconnected world, the G-7, G-8, and G-20 have emerged as crucial platforms for crisis management and global economic coordination. These groups, comprising the world's major economies, play a pivotal role in shaping economic policies and governance, addressing global challenges, and fostering international cooperation.

The Economic Importance and The Future of the G-7, G-8, and G-20

The G-7, G-8, and G-20 have been instrumental in promoting economic stability and growth. These forums bring together economists and diplomats from leading nations to discuss and coordinate policies that impact the global economy. As emerging economies and regional blocs gain prominence, the future of these groups is being reevaluated to ensure their continued relevance and effectiveness.

The impact of G-7, G-8, and G-20 on international trade and globalization

The G-7, G-8, and G-20 have a significant influence on international trade and globalization. Through their discussions and agreements, these groups shape trade policies, resolve disputes, and promote open markets. They also work towards reducing trade barriers and fostering economic cooperation, enabling a more integrated and interconnected global economy.

The role of G-7, G-8, and G-20 in addressing global economic inequality and poverty

Addressing global economic inequality and poverty is a pressing concern, and the G-7, G-8, and G-20 play a vital role in combating these challenges. These platforms allow for the exchange of ideas and the development of policies that aim to reduce inequality, promote inclusive growth, and alleviate poverty in both developed and developing nations.

The influence of G-7, G-8, and G-20 on global financial stability and regulation

Global financial stability and regulation are critical for a healthy and resilient global economy. The G-7, G-8, and G-20 serve as important forums for coordinating policies and regulations to ensure financial stability, prevent crises, and enhance the resilience of financial systems worldwide. These groups work towards establishing international standards and frameworks that promote responsible financial practices and safeguard against systemic risks.

The environmental sustainability agenda of G-7, G-8, and G-20 and its impact on future economic development

Recognizing the significant impact of climate change and environmental degradation on economic development, the G-7, G-8, and G-20 have placed environmental sustainability high on their agenda. By promoting sustainable practices, renewable energy, and climate change mitigation efforts, these groups strive to strike a balance between economic growth and environmental preservation.

The role of G-7, G-8, and G-20 in shaping global economic policies and governance

As key players in global economic governance, the G-7, G-8, and G-20 have the power to shape global economic policies. Through their discussions, agreements, and initiatives, these groups work towards fostering cooperation, coordination, and consensus on critical economic issues, ensuring a more stable and prosperous global economy.

The importance of G-7, G-8, and G-20 in promoting innovation and technological advancements

Technological advancements and innovation are crucial drivers of economic growth and development. The G-7, G-8, and G-20 recognize the importance of promoting innovation and technological advancements. Through collaborative efforts, these groups work towards fostering research and development, promoting entrepreneurship, and facilitating the transfer of technology, thereby driving economic progress and competitiveness.

The future prospects of G-7, G-8, and G-20 in light of emerging economies and regional blocs

With the rise of emerging economies and regional blocs, the future prospects of the G-7, G-8, and G-20 are evolving. These groups need to adapt and accommodate the changing global economic landscape, ensuring the inclusion and representation of a diverse range of countries. This will be crucial to maintain their effectiveness and legitimacy in addressing global economic challenges.

The potential challenges and opportunities for G-7, G-8, and G-20 in a post-pandemic world

The COVID-19 pandemic has highlighted the need for international cooperation and coordination in crisis management. The G-7, G-8, and G-20 face the challenge of addressing the economic fallout from the pandemic and designing strategies for recovery. However, this crisis also presents an opportunity for these groups to reevaluate their roles and priorities, strengthen global health systems, and promote resilient and sustainable economic growth.

The role of G-7, G-8, and G-20 in addressing global health crises and pandemics

Global health crises and pandemics require a coordinated and comprehensive response. The G-7, G-8, and G-20 play a crucial role in addressing these challenges by facilitating the exchange of information, resources, and expertise. These groups work towards strengthening global health systems, promoting research and development in healthcare, and ensuring access to affordable and equitable healthcare services for all.

The implications of G-7, G-8, and G-20 on regional economic integration and cooperation

The G-7, G-8, and G-20 have significant implications for regional economic integration and cooperation. Through their policies, agreements, and initiatives, these groups foster economic integration, promote regional cooperation, and support the development of regional trade blocs. They also provide a platform for regional economies to engage with the global economic governance framework, ensuring their interests and concerns are taken into account.

In conclusion, the G-7, G-8, and G-20 have a crucial role to play in crisis management and global economic coordination. These platforms bring together economists and diplomats to address economic challenges, promote cooperation, and shape policies that impact the global economy. As the world evolves, these groups must adapt to emerging economies, regional blocs, and new challenges such as pandemics and environmental sustainability to ensure a prosperous and sustainable future for all.

The Challenges of Ensuring Effective Global Economic Governance through G-7, G-8, and G-20

As economists and diplomats continue to navigate the complex landscape of global economic governance, the role of institutions such as the G-7, G-8, and G-20 has become increasingly significant. These forums provide a platform for world leaders to discuss and coordinate policies on key economic issues. However, there are several challenges that must be addressed to ensure effective global economic governance through these institutions.

One of the primary challenges is the economic importance and future of the G-7, G-8, and G-20. With emerging economies gaining prominence on the global stage, there is a need to reassess the composition and relevance of these forums. The inclusion of countries such as China, India, and Brazil in the G-20 reflects the shifting balance of economic power and the need for a more inclusive decision-making process.

Another challenge lies in the impact of these forums on international trade and globalization. While the G-7, G-8, and G-20 have played a crucial role in promoting free trade and open markets, they must also address the concerns of developing nations and ensure that the benefits of globalization are distributed more equitably.

Furthermore, the role of these institutions in addressing global economic inequality and poverty is of paramount importance. Despite progress in reducing poverty, income disparities persist both within and between countries. The G-7, G-8, and G-20 must prioritize policies that promote inclusive growth and address the root causes of inequality.

Moreover, the influence of these forums on global financial stability and regulation cannot be underestimated. In the wake of the 2008 financial crisis, there is a need for stronger international cooperation in overseeing financial markets and ensuring the stability of the global financial system.

The environmental sustainability agenda of the G-7, G-8, and G-20 is another critical challenge. As the world grapples with the consequences of climate change, these forums must take the lead in formulating policies that promote sustainable development and mitigate the impact of environmental degradation on future economic growth.

Furthermore, the role of the G-7, G-8, and G-20 in shaping global economic policies and governance cannot be overlooked. These forums have the potential to set the agenda for international economic cooperation and provide a platform for dialogue and collaboration among nations.

Additionally, the importance of these forums in promoting innovation and technological advancements cannot be overstated. As the world becomes increasingly interconnected and technology-driven, the G-7, G-8, and G-20 must foster an environment conducive to innovation and ensure that technological advancements benefit all countries.

Looking ahead, the future prospects of the G-7, G-8, and G-20 in light of emerging economies and regional blocs pose both challenges and opportunities. As regional organizations gain influence, these forums must adapt and collaborate with other institutions to effectively address global economic challenges.

Moreover, the potential challenges and opportunities for the G-7, G-8, and G-20 in a post-pandemic world cannot be ignored. The COVID-19 pandemic has exposed vulnerabilities in the global economic system, and these forums must play a crucial role in coordinating economic recovery efforts and preparing for future health crises.

Lastly, the implications of the G-7, G-8, and G-20 on regional economic integration and cooperation are significant. These forums must work closely with regional organizations to promote economic integration and foster cooperation on regional economic issues.

In conclusion, the challenges of ensuring effective global economic governance through the G-7, G-8, and G-20 are multifaceted and require continuous adaptation and collaboration. As economists and diplomats work towards addressing these challenges, it is crucial to recognize the importance of these forums in shaping the future of global economic policies and governance.

Chapter 7: The Importance of G-7, G-8, and G-20 in Promoting Innovation and Technological Advancements

G-7, G-8, and G-20 Initiatives for Research and Development Investments

In an increasingly interconnected and globalized world, research and development (R&D) investments play a crucial role in driving economic growth, promoting innovation, and addressing pressing global challenges. The G-7, G-8, and G-20, as prominent forums for economic cooperation, have recognized the importance of R&D investments in shaping the future of global economic governance.

These forums have consistently emphasized the significance of fostering innovation and technological advancements. They have recognized that R&D investments are essential for enhancing productivity, competitiveness, and sustainable economic development. To this end, the G-7, G-8, and G-20 have implemented various initiatives to promote R&D investments and collaboration among member countries.

One notable initiative is the establishment of research and innovation funds, such as the G-7 Science and Technology Ministers' meetings and the G-20 Innovation 20 (I-20) engagement group. These platforms provide opportunities for member countries to share best practices, exchange knowledge, and enhance cooperation in research and development. They also facilitate the creation of partnerships between governments, academia, and the private sector to promote research and innovation.

Furthermore, the G-7, G-8, and G-20 have recognized the need to address global challenges through R&D investments. For instance, they have focused on promoting sustainable development and environmental sustainability by investing in clean energy technologies, renewable resources, and climate change mitigation strategies. These initiatives aim to foster a transition to a low-carbon economy and promote sustainable economic growth.

The G-7, G-8, and G-20 have also recognized the importance of investing in health research and development, particularly in the wake of global health crises and pandemics. They have emphasized the need for coordinated efforts to address public health challenges, enhance healthcare systems, and develop vaccines and treatments. These initiatives aim to strengthen global health security and ensure effective responses to future health crises.

In conclusion, the G-7, G-8, and G-20 have demonstrated their commitment to promoting research and development investments as a key driver of economic growth, innovation, and global cooperation. Through various initiatives, these forums have facilitated the exchange of knowledge, fostered partnerships, and addressed pressing global challenges. However, in a rapidly changing global landscape, the future prospects of the G-7, G-8, and G-20 in promoting R&D investments will depend on their ability to adapt to emerging economies, regional blocs, and post-pandemic challenges. Nevertheless, their role in shaping global economic policies, addressing inequality and poverty, ensuring financial stability, and promoting sustainable development remains crucial for the future of global economic governance.

The Role of G-7, G-8, and G-20 in Fostering Technological Collaboration

Technological collaboration plays a crucial role in driving economic growth, innovation, and development in today's interconnected world. As economists and diplomats, it is essential to understand the role of global economic governance institutions like the G-7, G-8, and G-20 in fostering such collaboration and promoting technological advancements.

The G-7, G-8, and G-20 have been instrumental in shaping global economic policies and governance, including those related to technology. These forums bring together the world's leading economies, allowing for discussions and cooperation on various issues, including technological advancements.

One of the key ways in which these institutions foster technological collaboration is through knowledge sharing and information exchange. By bringing together experts, policymakers, and industry leaders from different countries, the G-7, G-8, and G-20 facilitate the sharing of best practices, experiences, and research findings. This exchange of knowledge helps countries learn from each other's successes and failures, enabling them to develop more effective strategies for technological development.

Furthermore, these forums also provide a platform for countries to collaborate on research and development projects. By pooling resources and expertise, nations can undertake joint initiatives that aim to address global challenges and foster technological advancements. These collaborative efforts can lead to breakthroughs in various fields, such as healthcare, clean energy, and digital technologies.

The G-7, G-8, and G-20 also play a crucial role in promoting innovation and entrepreneurship. Through their discussions and policy frameworks, these institutions create an enabling environment for businesses and startups to flourish. They emphasize the importance of research and development, intellectual property rights, and access to financing, all of which are essential for driving technological innovation.

Moreover, the G-7, G-8, and G-20 can leverage their collective economic power to support and promote emerging technologies. By aligning their policies and investments, these forums can facilitate the adoption and diffusion of new technologies, helping countries bridge the technological divide and achieve sustainable development.

In conclusion, the G-7, G-8, and G-20 have a vital role to play in fostering technological collaboration. Through knowledge sharing, research collaboration, and policy frameworks, these institutions promote innovation, support entrepreneurship, and drive technological advancements. As economists and diplomats, it is imperative to recognize the importance of these forums in shaping global economic policies and governance to ensure a prosperous and technologically advanced future for all nations.

The Impact of G-7, G-8, and G-20 on Global Innovation Ecosystems

In today's interconnected world, global economic governance plays a crucial role in shaping the future of innovation and technological advancements. This subchapter aims to explore the impact of G-7, G-8, and G-20 on global innovation ecosystems, with particular emphasis on the audience of economists and diplomats.

The Economic Importance and The Future of the G-7, G-8, and G-20

The G-7, G-8, and G-20 are key international forums that bring together the world's most advanced economies to discuss and coordinate policies on global economic issues. These forums serve as platforms for promoting innovation and technological advancements, which are vital for economic growth and competitiveness in the 21st century. As emerging economies and regional blocs gain prominence, the future of the G-7, G-8, and G-20 lies in their ability to adapt, include diverse perspectives, and address the changing global economic landscape.

The importance of G-7, G-8, and G-20 in promoting innovation and technological advancements

The G-7, G-8, and G-20 play a significant role in promoting innovation by facilitating knowledge exchange, fostering collaboration among member countries, and supporting research and development initiatives. They provide a platform for sharing best practices, identifying common challenges, and exploring opportunities for cooperation in emerging fields such as artificial intelligence, biotechnology, and renewable energy. By promoting innovation, these forums contribute to economic growth, job creation, and the overall advancement of societies.

The environmental sustainability agenda of G-7, G-8, and G-20 and its impact on future economic development

As the world faces pressing environmental challenges, the G-7, G-8, and G-20 have recognized the need for sustainable development and the transition to a low-carbon economy. These forums have played a crucial role in setting environmental agendas, promoting clean technologies, and mobilizing resources for climate action. By prioritizing sustainability, they not only address environmental concerns but also create new opportunities for innovation and economic growth in sectors such as renewable energy, green infrastructure, and sustainable agriculture.

The future prospects of G-7, G-8, and G-20 in light of emerging economies and regional blocs

The rise of emerging economies and regional blocs presents both opportunities and challenges for the G-7, G-8, and G-20. While these forums have traditionally represented the most advanced economies, engaging with emerging economies is crucial for addressing global economic inequality, promoting inclusive growth, and harnessing the potential of diverse perspectives. Collaboration with regional blocs can also enhance global economic integration, foster cooperation, and create synergies for innovation and technological advancements.

In conclusion, the impact of G-7, G-8, and G-20 on global innovation ecosystems is significant. These forums promote innovation, drive technological advancements, address sustainability challenges, and shape global economic policies. As the world continues to evolve, it is essential for economists and diplomats to closely examine the role of G-7, G-8, and G-20 in promoting innovation, adapting to emerging economies, and addressing global challenges to ensure a sustainable and prosperous future for all.

Challenges and Opportunities for G-7, G-8, and G-20 in Nurturing Technological Progress

In today's rapidly evolving global landscape, technological progress has become a driving force behind economic growth and development. As economists and diplomats, it is crucial to understand the challenges and opportunities that G-7, G-8, and G-20 face in nurturing technological progress.

One of the major challenges faced by these international forums is the increasing competition from emerging economies and regional blocs. As countries like China, India, and Brazil continue to invest heavily in research and development, they are rapidly catching up with the technological advancements of traditional G-7 and G-8 members. This poses a challenge for G-7, G-8, and G-20 to maintain their leadership in technological innovation.

However, this challenge also presents an opportunity for collaboration and knowledge-sharing. G-7, G-8, and G-20 can leverage their collective expertise and resources to foster collaboration between developed and emerging economies. By promoting international partnerships and technology transfers, these forums can help bridge the technological gap and create a more inclusive and equitable global innovation ecosystem.

Another challenge lies in addressing the ethical and social implications of technological progress. As new technologies such as artificial intelligence, automation, and biotechnology continue to advance, they bring forth concerns regarding job displacement, privacy, and inequality. G-7, G-8, and G-20 have a crucial role in ensuring that technological progress is guided by ethical principles and benefits all members of society. By establishing regulatory frameworks and promoting responsible innovation, these forums can mitigate the negative consequences of technological advancements.

Furthermore, G-7, G-8, and G-20 have the opportunity to shape global economic policies and governance to foster technological progress. By advocating for open markets, free trade, and intellectual property rights protection, these forums can create an enabling environment for innovation. Additionally, they can support research and development initiatives by providing funding and infrastructure, thus nurturing technological progress at both national and international levels.

In a post-pandemic world, G-7, G-8, and G-20 face the challenge of reviving economies and promoting sustainable recovery. Technological progress will play a crucial role in this process, as it offers new avenues for economic diversification and resilience. By prioritizing investments in digital infrastructure, promoting digital literacy, and fostering digital transformation, these forums can facilitate economic recovery and ensure long-term prosperity.

In conclusion, G-7, G-8, and G-20 have a vital role in nurturing technological progress. By addressing challenges such as competition from emerging economies, ethical implications, and fostering collaboration, these forums can harness the opportunities presented by technological advancements. As economists and diplomats, it is imperative to recognize the importance of technology in shaping the global economic landscape and work towards leveraging its potential for inclusive and sustainable development.

Chapter 8: The Future Prospects of G-7, G-8, and G-20 in Light of Emerging Economies and Regional Blocs

G-7, G-8, and G-20's Engagement with Emerging Economies

The global economic landscape has undergone significant changes over the years, with the emergence of new economic powerhouses in the form of emerging economies. As the world grapples with the challenges posed by globalization, international trade, and economic inequality, the role of international forums such as the G-7, G-8, and G-20 in engaging with these emerging economies becomes crucial.

One of the key areas where the G-7, G-8, and G-20 have engaged with emerging economies is international trade and globalization. These forums have recognized the economic importance of emerging economies and have worked towards fostering greater cooperation, promoting trade liberalization, and reducing barriers to entry. By engaging with emerging economies, the G-7, G-8, and G-20 have played a significant role in shaping global trade policies, creating opportunities for economic growth, and fostering a more interconnected and inclusive global economy.

Moreover, the G-7, G-8, and G-20 have also recognized the need to address global economic inequality and poverty. By engaging with emerging economies, these forums have sought to promote inclusive growth and development, bridging the gap between the developed and developing world. Through various initiatives, including financial assistance, capacity building, and knowledge sharing, the G-7, G-8, and G-20 have played a vital role in reducing poverty and promoting economic empowerment.

In addition, the G-7, G-8, and G-20 have worked towards ensuring global financial stability and regulation. By engaging with emerging economies, these forums have sought to strengthen the global financial system, enhance regulatory frameworks, and promote financial inclusion. Through cooperation and coordination, the G-7, G-8, and G-20 have played a crucial role in mitigating financial risks and ensuring the stability of the global economy.

Furthermore, the G-7, G-8, and G-20 have recognized the importance of environmental sustainability and its impact on future economic development. By engaging with emerging economies, these forums have promoted sustainable development practices, renewable energy, and climate change mitigation. Through collaborative efforts, the G-7, G-8, and G-20 have fostered a global environmental agenda, addressing the challenges of climate change and promoting a greener and more sustainable future.

Looking ahead, the future prospects of the G-7, G-8, and G-20 in light of emerging economies and regional blocs are promising. These forums have increasingly recognized the importance of engaging with emerging economies and have expanded their membership to include key players from these regions. By embracing a more inclusive approach, the G-7, G-8, and G-20 can leverage the economic potential of emerging economies and strengthen global economic governance.

However, the G-7, G-8, and G-20 also face potential challenges and opportunities in a post-pandemic world. The COVID-19 pandemic has highlighted the need for stronger global health governance and coordination. The role of the G-7, G-8, and G-20 in addressing global health crises and pandemics will become even more critical in the future.

Furthermore, the implications of the G-7, G-8, and G-20 on regional economic integration and cooperation cannot be overlooked. These forums have the potential to shape regional trade agreements, enhance cross-border investments, and promote economic integration. By engaging with emerging economies and regional blocs, the G-7, G-8, and G-20 can foster greater regional cooperation and contribute to a more interconnected and prosperous world.

In conclusion, the G-7, G-8, and G-20's engagement with emerging economies plays a vital role in shaping global economic governance. From addressing economic inequality and poverty to promoting financial stability, environmental sustainability, and innovation, these forums have the potential to drive positive change in the world economy. However, they must also navigate the challenges and opportunities presented by a post-pandemic world and the implications of regional economic integration. By embracing a collaborative and inclusive approach, the G-7, G-8, and G-20 can pave the way for a more prosperous and sustainable future.

The Role of G-7, G-8, and G-20 in Shaping Regional Economic Integration

In today's interconnected world, regional economic integration has become a critical aspect of global economic governance. Regional blocs and organizations play a significant role in shaping economic policies, promoting cooperation, and addressing common challenges. Among these organizations, the G-7, G-8, and G-20 have emerged as influential platforms for economic dialogue and decision-making. This subchapter explores the role of these groups in shaping regional economic integration and their impact on various aspects of global economic governance.

The G-7, consisting of Canada, France, Germany, Italy, Japan, the United Kingdom, and the United States, has traditionally been seen as the forum for major advanced economies to address global economic issues. However, with the inclusion of Russia, the G-8 expanded its reach and influence. The subsequent establishment of the G-20, which includes both developed and emerging economies, further enhanced the importance of these forums in shaping regional economic integration.

One of the key roles of the G-7, G-8, and G-20 is their impact on international trade and globalization. These groups provide a platform for member countries to negotiate trade agreements, address trade barriers, and promote free and fair trade practices. Through their discussions and agreements, they have played a significant role in shaping the rules and regulations governing global trade and investment.

Another area where these forums have made a considerable impact is in addressing global economic inequality and poverty. By bringing together the world's major economies, they have the potential to address issues such as income disparities, social inclusion, and poverty reduction. Through coordinated efforts and policy initiatives, they can foster economic growth and development, particularly in developing countries.

Furthermore, the G-7, G-8, and G-20 have a crucial role in ensuring global financial stability and regulation. These groups have been instrumental in coordinating responses to financial crises, strengthening regulatory frameworks, and promoting financial transparency. Their efforts have helped prevent and mitigate the impact of financial crises, ensuring the stability of the global financial system.

The environmental sustainability agenda is another key area where the G-7, G-8, and G-20 have made significant contributions. Recognizing the importance of sustainable development, these forums have promoted environmental protection, climate change mitigation, and the transition to a low-carbon economy. Their commitments and initiatives have influenced global environmental policies and shaped the future of economic development.

Moreover, the G-7, G-8, and G-20 play a vital role in shaping global economic policies and governance. Through their discussions and agreements, they set the agenda for global economic cooperation, addressing issues such as macroeconomic coordination, fiscal policies, and financial sector reforms. Their decisions and recommendations have a significant impact on the global economic landscape.

Additionally, these groups promote innovation and technological advancements. By facilitating cooperation among member countries, they foster research and development, knowledge sharing, and the adoption of new technologies. This promotes economic growth, increases productivity, and enhances competitiveness in the global marketplace.

Looking towards the future, the G-7, G-8, and G-20 face challenges and opportunities in a rapidly changing world. The emergence of new economies and regional blocs calls for greater inclusivity and representation in these forums. The post-pandemic world presents unique challenges, such as the need for coordinated responses to public health crises and the revival of economies. These groups need to adapt and evolve to effectively address these challenges and seize the opportunities presented by a changing global landscape.

In conclusion, the G-7, G-8, and G-20 play a crucial role in shaping regional economic integration and addressing various global economic challenges. From promoting free trade to addressing inequality, from ensuring financial stability to driving environmental sustainability, these forums have a significant impact on the global economic governance. However, they must continually adapt and evolve to effectively address emerging issues and include the perspectives of a changing global order.

G-7, G-8, and G-20's Collaborations with Regional Blocs

The G-7, G-8, and G-20, as leading global economic forums, have continuously sought to foster collaborations with regional blocs to address key economic challenges and promote sustainable development.

This subchapter explores the importance of these collaborations and their impact on various aspects of the global economy.

One of the key areas where the G-7, G-8, and G-20 have collaborated with regional blocs is in international trade and globalization. Recognizing the significance of regional trade agreements, these forums have actively engaged with regional blocs such as the European Union (EU), ASEAN, and Mercosur to promote trade liberalization and eliminate barriers to commerce. Through these collaborations, the G-7, G-8, and G-20 have played a crucial role in advancing global economic integration.

Moreover, the G-7, G-8, and G-20 have also focused on addressing global economic inequality and poverty through partnerships with regional blocs. By working with organizations like the African Union and the Association of Southeast Asian Nations (ASEAN), these forums have aimed to promote inclusive growth, reduce poverty, and foster sustainable development in regions that face economic challenges. These collaborations have not only helped in poverty alleviation but have also contributed to regional stability and security.

In the realm of global financial stability and regulation, the G-7, G-8, and G-20 have collaborated with regional blocs to enhance financial systems and prevent financial crises. By engaging with regional organizations such as the Financial Stability Board (FSB), the International Monetary Fund (IMF), and the World Bank, these forums have developed policies and regulations to ensure the stability of financial markets and promote responsible financial practices.

Additionally, the G-7, G-8, and G-20 have actively pursued environmental sustainability agendas in collaboration with regional blocs. Recognizing the urgent need to address climate change and promote sustainable development, these forums have partnered with regional organizations like the European Union and the Pacific Islands

Forum to advance global environmental goals. Through these collaborations, the G-7, G-8, and G-20 have worked towards mitigating the adverse effects of climate change and promoting green economic development.

In conclusion, the G-7, G-8, and G-20 have recognized the importance of collaborating with regional blocs to address global economic challenges comprehensively. Through partnerships in areas such as international trade, poverty alleviation, financial stability, environmental sustainability, and more, these forums have played a vital role in shaping global economic policies and governance. As the world continues to evolve, the G-7, G-8, and G-20 must adapt and strengthen their collaborations with emerging economies and regional blocs to ensure their continued relevance and effectiveness in a rapidly changing global landscape.

Challenges and Opportunities for G-7,

Challenges and Opportunities for G-7

As we analyze the challenges and opportunities facing the G-7, it is crucial to recognize the group's significance in global economic governance. Comprising the world's most advanced economies, the G-7 – consisting of Canada, France, Germany, Italy, Japan, the United Kingdom, and the United States – has played a pivotal role in shaping international economic policies and fostering cooperation among nations. However, in an ever-changing global landscape, the G-7 faces several challenges and opportunities that demand attention.

One of the primary challenges for the G-7 is adapting to the changing dynamics of the global economy. Emerging economies and regional blocs are gaining prominence and influence, altering the traditional power dynamics within the global economic governance structure. The G-7 must find ways to integrate and collaborate with these emerging economies, recognizing their contributions while also maintaining their own relevance and influence.

Another significant challenge lies in addressing global economic inequality and poverty. The G-7 has a responsibility to ensure that economic growth is inclusive and benefits all segments of society, particularly the marginalized and vulnerable populations. By implementing policies that prioritize equitable development, the G-7 can play a crucial role in reducing poverty and narrowing the wealth gap on a global scale.

Financial stability and regulation are also areas where the G-7 faces challenges. The group must continue to strengthen global financial institutions and regulatory frameworks to prevent future financial crises. Furthermore, the G-7 must adapt to the evolving financial landscape, including the rise of digital currencies and the increasing integration of technology in financial services.

The G-7 has an opportunity to lead the charge in environmental sustainability. As the world faces the urgent threat of climate change, the G-7 can drive the agenda for sustainable development and promote green innovation. By setting ambitious targets and implementing effective policies, the G-7 can influence the future of economic development while mitigating environmental risks.

In a post-pandemic world, the G-7 must navigate new challenges and opportunities. The group can play a crucial role in coordinating global efforts to rebuild economies, ensuring a resilient and equitable recovery. Additionally, the G-7 has an opportunity to strengthen global health governance, addressing health crises and pandemics through improved international cooperation and coordination.

Lastly, the G-7's influence on regional economic integration and cooperation cannot be overlooked. By fostering dialogue and collaboration, the G-7 can contribute to the development of regional blocs and enhance trade relations among nations.

In conclusion, the challenges and opportunities facing the G-7 are vast and complex. However, with a proactive and inclusive approach, the G-7 can continue to shape global economic policies, address inequality and poverty, promote financial stability, champion environmental sustainability, and play a pivotal role in global health and regional economic integration. As economists and diplomats, it is imperative that we recognize the importance of the G-7 and strive to support its efforts to build a more prosperous and sustainable world.